GEOFACTS

WITHDRAWN

MOUNTAIN
GEO FACTS

Izzi Howell

Crabtree Publishing Company
www.crabtreebooks.com

Crabtree Publishing Company
www.crabtreebooks.com
1-800-387-7650

Published in Canada
Crabtree Publishing
616 Welland Avenue
St. Catharines, ON
L2M 5V6

Published in the United States
Crabtree Publishing
PMB 59051
350 Fifth Ave, 59th Floor
New York, NY 10118

Published in 2018 by CRABTREE PUBLISHING COMPANY.

First published in 2017 by The Watts Publishing Group
Copyright © The Watts Publishing Group 2017

Author: Izzi Howell

Editors: Izzi Howell, Ellen Rodger

Design: Rocket Design (East Anglia) Ltd

Editorial director: Kathy Middleton

Proofreader: Angela Kaelberer

Prepress technician: Abigail Smith

Print and production coordinator: Margaret Amy Salter

Photographs

Alamy: Extreme Sports Photo 19b, Alan Gignoux 29b; iStock: bravobravo 7bl, jack0m 9bl, JTSorrell 11tl, jeremkin 15tl, andyKRAKOVSKI 15br, fotoVoyager 18b, JeffGoulden 22b, johnnya123 23t, sihasakprachum 26b, dibrova 27tc, Skouatroulio 27tb, viti 28c, dzubanovska 29t; Peter Bull 4-5, 19t, 20; Shutterstock: skelos 5t, 12t, 21l and 22t, fluidworkshop 6t, BlueRingMedia 7t, Arthur Balitskiy 7br, Matthijs Wetterauw 9tl, Darren J. Bradley 9tc, Chris Warham 9tr, Juergen Wackenhut 9br, Designua 10t, 10b, 11c and 17bl, iQoncept 10c, Krishna.Wu 11tr, Ecuadorpostales 13tl, Mossia 13b, Athanasia Nomikou 14, Francois Arseneault 15tr, Macrovector 15bl, chaoss 16tl, Venturelli Luca 16tr, Red monkey 16bl, corlaffra 17tr, URRRA 18t, Sopotnicki 21tr, Felix Lipov 21cr, StockPhotoAstur 21br, Sunny_nsk 23bl, Robert Biedermann 23cr, Tomacco 23br, Byelikova Oksana 24t, robuart 24b, Shirstok 25t, Seita 25b, Benjavisa Ruangvaree 26t, Daniel Prudek 27t, Sentavio 27bl, Allies Interactive 27br, Adazhiy Dmytro 28t, Krylovochka 28b; Techtype: 6b, 8t and 12b.

All design elements from Shutterstock: Meilun, Meowu, StockSmartStart, Blablo101, TyBy, GoodVector, DVARG, VectorShow, Oksana Alekseeva, SeneGal, Jane Kelly, polunoch and lamnee.

Every attempt has been made to clear copyright. Should there be any inadvertent omission, please apply to the publisher for rectification.

Printed in the USA/122019/BG20171102

Library and Archives Canada Cataloguing in Publication

Howell, Izzi, author
    Mountain geo facts / Izzi Howell.

(Geo facts)
Includes index.
Issued in print and electronic formats.
ISBN 978-0-7787-4384-2 (hardcover).--
ISBN 978-0-7787-4406-1 (softcover).--
ISBN 978-1-4271-2017-5 (HTML)

    1. Mountain ecology--Juvenile literature. 2. Mountains--Juvenile literature. I. Title.

QH541.5.M65H69 2018   j577.5'3   C2017-906905-5
                                           C2017-906906-3

Library of Congress Cataloging-in Publication Data

Names: Howell, Izzi, author.
Title: Mountain geo facts / Izzi Howell.
Description: New York, NY : Crabtree Publishing Company, 2018. |
Series: Geo facts | Includes index. |
Identifiers: LCCN 2017050654 (print) | LCCN 2017052111 (ebook) |
  ISBN 9781427120175 (Electronic HTML) |
  ISBN 9780778743842 (reinforced library binding) |
  ISBN 9780778744061 (pbk.)
Subjects: LCSH: Mountains--Juvenile literature. | Mountain ecology--
  Juvenile literature.
Classification: LCC GB512 (ebook) | LCC GB512 .H68 2018 (print) |
DDC 551.43/2--dc23
LC record available at https://lccn.loc.gov/2017050654

Contents

What is a Mountain?

Mountains are high, rocky areas of land with steep, sloped sides. They are found on every continent on Earth. There are even mountains deep under the sea.

Mountains

There is no official minimum height for a mountain. However, most people would use the word mountain to describe an area that rises dramatically higher than **sea level** and its surroundings. The bottom part of a mountain is called the base and the top is called the **peak** or summit.

peak

base
sea level

Mountain ranges

Mountains are millions of years old. The way in which mountains are created (see pages 8–11) means that they often form in groups, known as ranges. Well-known mountain ranges across the world include the Himalayas in Asia, the Alps in Europe, the Andes in South America, and the Rocky Mountains in North America.

FOCUS ON **The Rocky Mountains** (page 22)

mountain ranges

FOCUS ON **The Appalachian Mountains** (page 29)

FOCUS ON **The Andes** (page 12)

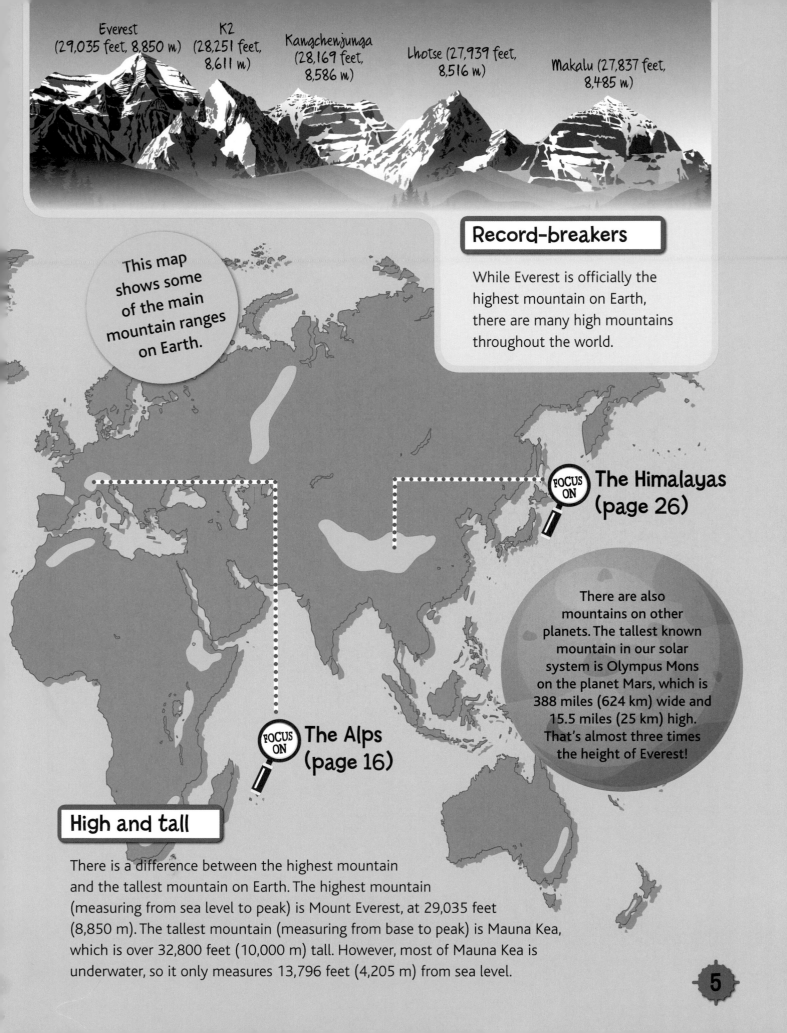

Everest (29,035 feet, 8,850 m)

K2 (28,251 feet, 8,611 m)

Kangchenjunga (28,169 feet, 8,586 m)

Lhotse (27,939 feet, 8,516 m)

Makalu (27,837 feet, 8,485 m)

This map shows some of the main mountain ranges on Earth.

Record-breakers

While Everest is officially the highest mountain on Earth, there are many high mountains throughout the world.

FOCUS ON **The Himalayas** (page 26)

There are also mountains on other planets. The tallest known mountain in our solar system is Olympus Mons on the planet Mars, which is 388 miles (624 km) wide and 15.5 miles (25 km) high. That's almost three times the height of Everest!

FOCUS ON **The Alps** (page 16)

High and tall

There is a difference between the highest mountain and the tallest mountain on Earth. The highest mountain (measuring from sea level to peak) is Mount Everest, at 29,035 feet (8,850 m). The tallest mountain (measuring from base to peak) is Mauna Kea, which is over 32,800 feet (10,000 m) tall. However, most of Mauna Kea is underwater, so it only measures 13,796 feet (4,205 m) from sea level.

Moving Plates

Earth is made up of different layers of solid and liquid rock and metal. The movement of the outer layer creates mountains on the surface of Earth.

Inside Earth

There are four main layers inside Earth. At the very center is the inner core, which is made of solid iron. The outer core is a layer of liquid iron and nickel. The third layer is the **mantle**, which is composed of semi-molten rock (**magma**). The outermost layer, or **crust**, is made of solid rock.

Crust – between 3.1 and 43 miles (5 and 70 km) thick

Mantle – 1,864 miles (3,000 km) thick

Outer core – 1,242 miles (2,000 km) thick

Inner core – 745 miles (1,200 km) thick

The boundary between the inner and outer **core** can reach temperatures of 10,832 °Fahrenheit (6,000 °C), which is as hot as the surface of the Sun!

Plates

Earth's crust is split into huge pieces of solid rock called **tectonic plates**. The plates are made up of two types of crust: continental and oceanic. **Continental plates** lie under the continents in shallow water along some coasts. **Oceanic plates** are found under the ocean. They are thinner but **denser** than continental plates. The area where plates meet is a boundary. Mountains, volcanoes, and earthquakes are common at **plate boundaries**.

If you placed the east coast of South America and the west coast of Africa next to each other, they would roughly fit together. This is because they were once part of the same continent. Over millions of years, the continent split apart because of the movement of plates.

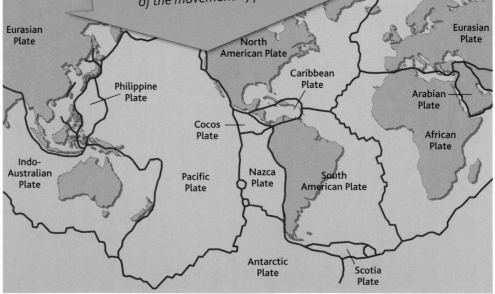

This map shows Earth's major tectonic plates.

Eurasian Plate

North American Plate

Caribbean Plate

Arabian Plate

Philippine Plate

Cocos Plate

African Plate

Indo-Australian Plate

Pacific Plate

Nazca Plate

South American Plate

Eurasian Plate

Antarctic Plate

Scotia Plate

Convection currents

Magma in the mantle is heated by the high temperature of Earth's core. This causes **convection currents**, or movement in liquids caused by heat. The hot, semi-molten magma rises up while cool magma sinks toward the center.

You can see convection currents when you heat water in a pot. The water closest to the heat source bubbles to the surface, while cooler water sinks down to the bottom.

Moving plates

The movement of the magma in the mantle makes the oceanic and continental plates slowly shift location. They travel a few inches (cm) every year. However, over millions of years, the movement of plates can make continents shift thousands of miles (km) apart. This movement led to the separation of South America and Africa (see page 6).

Types of movement

Plates move in three different ways. They can move toward each other, away from each other, or slide past each other. The way in which plates move toward and away from each other creates mountains, volcanoes, and earthquakes.

This canyon is at the boundary between the Eurasian and North American plates in Iceland. It was formed by the plates moving away from each other.

plates moving away from each other

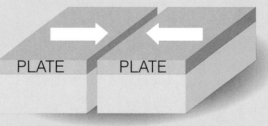

plates moving toward each other

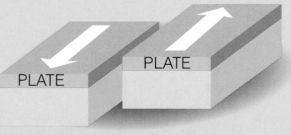

plates moving past each other

7

Fold and Block Mountains

Fold and block mountains are created when plates move towards each other. Some of the largest mountain ranges in the world, such as the Alps, Himalayas, and Andes, are fold mountains.

Fold formation

When two plates move toward each other, the crust between them is pushed upward. This tends to happen between continental plates. The **compression** of the crust makes it crease and fold. You can observe the same effect if you push the edges of a tablecloth together, creating ripples in the center.

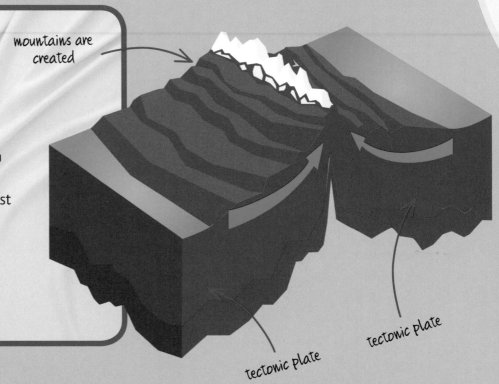

mountains are created

tectonic plate

tectonic plate

Folded ranges

At first, the crust is pushed into small folds. Over millions of years, the compression gets greater. Larger and deeper folds are created. This leads to the creation of vast mountain ranges such as the Himalayas.

Microscopic fossilized seashells have been found near the summit of Everest. This is because the land at the peak of Everest was once underneath the ocean. The land was pushed to its current height by tectonic forces.

Types of folds

We can observe different types of fold in the layers of rock that make up the Earth's crust. Most fold mountains have more than one type of fold. Curved, up-and-down folds are the most common. However, the layers can also be folded in a zigzag shape or all slanted in one direction.

Some plates fold down when compression is applied, creating a U-shaped fold.

Upside-down, U-shaped folds are created when both sides of the rock are pushed inward.

Zigzag folds have straight folds with no curves.

Block mountains

When Earth's crust breaks apart along a fault line, it forms several separate blocks of land. When tectonic forces push one block of land upward and the blocks on either side downward, it creates a block mountain.

These block mountains are in the Black Forest, Germany. They were pushed up along fault lines by tectonic forces. A small village was built on the low, flat valley in between the mountains.

block mountain

block mountain

Volcanic Mountains

Many mountains around the world are or once were volcanoes. Volcanoes are places where hot magma from the mantle erupts through the surface of the Earth.

Underwater

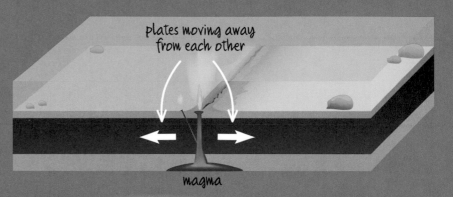

plates moving away from each other

magma

Volcanoes are often created underwater when two oceanic plates move away from each other. Magma from the mantle rises up to fill the gap in between the plates.

Hotspots

Volcanoes also form in volcanic hotspots where the oceanic crust is very thin and easily melted by magma from the mantle. When the oceanic crust melts, more magma from the mantle breaks through, creating an underwater volcano that grows larger with each eruption.

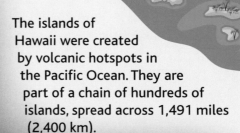

The islands of Hawaii were created by volcanic hotspots in the Pacific Ocean. They are part of a chain of hundreds of islands, spread across 1,491 miles (2,400 km).

Meeting plates

Volcanoes also occur along boundaries where oceanic and continental plates meet. When an oceanic plate collides with a continental plate, the denser oceanic plate is pushed underneath the continental plate. The oceanic plate is forced down into the mantle, where it melts into magma. This extra magma rises up to the surface of the continental plate, where it bursts out as a volcano.

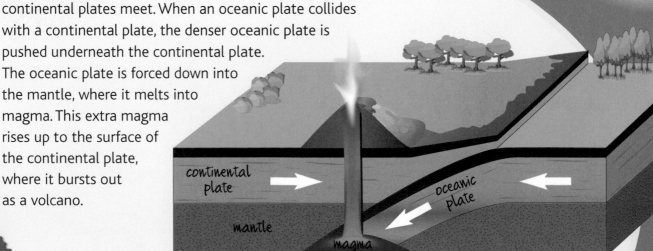

continental plate

oceanic plate

mantle

magma

Types of volcanoes

Most people think of volcanoes as cone-shaped mountains. However, volcanoes can have many different shapes, depending on the amount and direction of **lava** flow.

Shield volcanoes are the largest type of volcano. They have gently sloping sides. They are formed by runny lava, which flows quickly across the land.

Stratovolcanoes have steep sides, formed from thick lava. The lava cannot flow far before it hardens, so it builds up on the side of the mountain.

Mauna Kea in Hawaii is a shield volcano.

Mount Fuji in Japan is a stratovolcano.

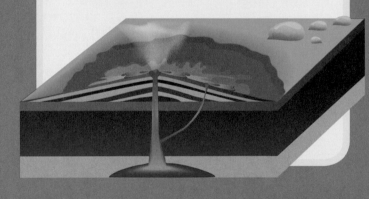

Extinct volcanoes

An **extinct** volcano will never erupt again. Scientists can predict if a volcano is extinct by measuring the amount of magma under the surface. If there is very little magma, the volcano is extinct. Some volcanoes are **dormant**, which means that it is unlikely, but not impossible, that they will erupt again.

There is a massive dormant volcano under Yellowstone National Park in Wyoming. It hasn't erupted for 630,000 years. If it erupts again, it will affect Earth's climate and its lava will cover a huge area of land!

FOCUS ON THE ANDES

The Andes are the longest mountain range on Earth. They stretch along the west coast of South America, from tropical Venezuela in the north to icy Patagonia in the south.

FACT FILE

LENGTH
5,530 miles (8,900 km)

HIGHEST POINT
22,831 feet (6,959 m)
Mount Aconcagua

COUNTRIES
Venezuela, Colombia, Ecuador, Peru, Bolivia, Chile, Argentina

Plate collision

The Andes were created millions of years ago, when the South American continental plate collided with the Nazca and Antarctic oceanic plates. The continental plate was pushed over the denser oceanic plate. This created many volcanic mountains.

3.1 to 3.9 inches (80 to 100 mm) of the Nazca plate is disappearing under the South American plate every year.

0 inch
(0 mm)

3.9 inch
(100 mm)

actual size

GUYANA
SURINAME
FRENCH GUIANA
VENEZUELA
COLOMBIA
Quito
Chimborazo
Equator
EQUADOR
Andes
BRAZIL
PERU
Lake Titicaca
BOLIVIA
Altiplano
PARAGUAY
Mount Aconcagua
CHILE
Ojos del Salado
Andes
URUGUAY
Pacific Ocean
ARGENTINA
Atlantic Ocean
Patagonia

12

Volcanic mountains

Most mountains along the Andes are volcanoes. Some of them have been extinct or dormant for many years. Others still erupt frequently. The world's highest active volcano, Ojos del Salado, which stands at 22,614 feet (6,893 m), is located in the Andes.

The eruption of the Cotopaxi volcano in the Andes in 2015 was visible 31 miles (50 km) away in Quito, the capital of Ecuador.

Altiplano

As well as steep mountains, there are high **plateaus** in the Andes, such as the Altiplano. The Altiplano is a flat, dry area mainly in Bolivia and Peru that reaches around 12,467 feet (3,800 m) above sea level. It was created very quickly, when tectonic forces lifted an area of the crust.

Chimborazo is a dormant volcano in the Andes, near the equator in Ecuador. Because Earth bulges at the equator, the peak of Chimborazo is actually further from the center of Earth than the peak of Mount Everest.

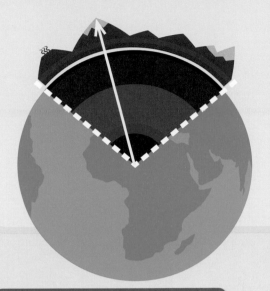

Mount Aconcagua

Not all mountains in the Andes are volcanoes. Mount Aconcagua, the highest mountain in the Andes and the highest mountain outside of Asia, is a fold mountain. However, Mount Aconcagua was also created by the same event that made the volcanoes along the Andes—the collision of the South American and Nazca plates.

Basins

There are several basins across the Altiplano. Lake Titicaca, the world's highest **navigable** lake, is located in a basin in the north of the plateau. In the south of the Altiplano, water has evaporated from basins that were once prehistoric lakes, leaving behind large flat areas covered in a thick crust of salt and minerals.

Changing Mountains

Mountains are always changing shape. Erosion and **landslides** cause parts of their rocky slopes to fall and wear away, giving them their characteristic jagged shape. **Glaciers** also carve deep valleys through mountainous areas.

Rock

The type of rock that a mountain is made from affects the speed at which it erodes. Areas of soft rock will erode more quickly than areas of hard rock.

In the past, the Appalachian Mountains were taller than the Himalayas, but after millions of years of **erosion**, they are now thousands of feet (m) shorter.

Water

Rain, rivers, and other forms of moving water can dramatically erode rock. Rain gets into cracks on the mountain slopes, breaking away chunks of rock. Rainwater that is not absorbed by the ground also flows down the side of the mountain, carrying particles of soil and small rocks with it. Most rivers begin in high, mountainous ground. They flow quickly downhill from their source, carving channels and valleys into the slopes.

Wind

Mountains are very windy, as there is nothing to block the wind at such great heights. Strong winds erode mountains by blowing away loose rock. Tiny pieces of rock are picked up by the wind and blown against the mountainside, further wearing away the slope.

Temperature changes

Rising and falling temperatures affect erosion. When the temperature drops below 32° Fahrenheit (0°C), any water that has fallen between rocks or been absorbed by the soil freezes solid. The frozen water expands, creating cracks in the rock and soil. When the temperature rises and the ice melts, these loose chunks of rock and soil easily fall away.

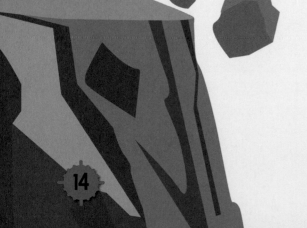

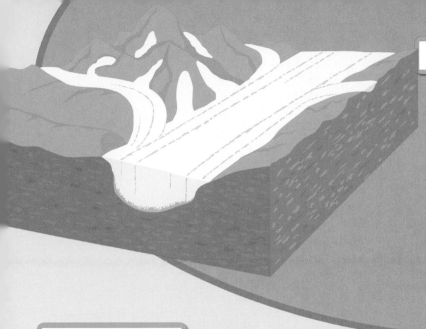

Glaciers

Slow moving rivers of ice, known as glaciers, are often found in high mountain ranges. The weight and force of the ice, as well as the rocks suspended in the glacier, cuts through the land. This creates U-shaped valleys at the base of mountains. In the past, Earth's climate was much colder, and there were many more glaciers than there are today. These glaciers, which have since melted, cut valleys out of the lower reaches of the mountains.

Landslides

Gravity will eventually pull any unsupported rock or mud down the side of a mountain. Heavy rains or strong winds can loosen large amounts of rock and mud. This material can fall all at once, as part of a landslide. The force and weight of the falling rock erodes the lower slopes as it makes its way down.

In this landslide, fallen rock from the peak of the mountain has nearly reached the base.

Caves

Some mountains have deep caves hidden inside them. These caves are usually carved out of the rock by water, which is absorbed through the ground and slowly wears away large, hollow underground spaces.

This cave inside a volcano was formed by magma. When a volcano becomes dormant, the tubes that the magma once flowed through are left empty.

FOCUS ON — The Alps

FACT FILE

LENGTH
745 mile (1,200 km)

HIGHEST POINT
15,780 feet (4,810 m)
Mont Blanc

COUNTRIES
France, Germany, Austria, Italy, Switzerland, Monaco, Liechtenstein, Slovenia

The Alps are a crescent-shaped mountain range in southern Europe. They are the biggest mountain range in Europe, stretching through eight countries.

Formation

The Alps are fold mountains. They were created when the African tectonic plate moved toward the Eurasian plate, pushing up the land in between into high mountain peaks. The same movement also formed the Pyrenees – a range of mountains on the border between France and Spain.

The peak of Mont Blanc is covered with a dome of ice in winter. This means that the mountain can measure up to 52 feet (16 m) higher in winter than in summer.

The Matterhorn

Originally, the Matterhorn mountain in the Alps had a rounded shape, like a hill. In summer, the ice that covers the high peak of the mountain melts and falls into cracks in the rock. In winter, the water freezes. This fractures, or breaks, the rock, which then falls off the mountain. Over millions of years, this cycle of erosion has changed the shape of the mountain from hill to pyramid.

Glaciers of the past

The Alps were home to many glaciers thousands of years ago, when Earth had a much colder climate. As the temperature increased over time, these glaciers melted, creating rivers and leaving behind large piles of rocks. However, some glaciers still exist in the Alps.

Disappearing glaciers

As Earth's temperature continues to increase due to climate change, the remaining glaciers in the Alps are in danger of disappearing. The melting of these glaciers could cause flooding, so scientists are trying to find ways to slow the melting down. One effective method is to cover the glaciers with white blankets in the summer. This stops the Sun's rays from hitting the glaciers and helps to keep them cool.

Causing an avalanche

Avalanches often happen after heavy snowfall. The weight of the heavy extra snow is so great that it slides down the mountain. As it falls, it picks up more snow, ice, and rocks from further down the mountain. Earthquakes regularly start avalanches. They can also be triggered by human activity, such as the vibrations caused by noise, skiing, and helicopters.

Avalanches

An **avalanche** is a large amount of snow, ice and rock that suddenly falls down a mountain. They are common in the Alps. Avalanches are one of the most dangerous and destructive events that can happen on a mountain. The weight and force of the falling snow can kill people and damage forests and buildings on its way down.

This photo shows an avalanche in the Alps. Snow from near the peak of the mountain slid downhill toward the base, leaving the bare rock exposed.

Deadly snow

In the winter of 1950-1, there were nearly 650 avalanches in the Alps, due to unusually heavy snow. This period is known as the Winter of Terror. Over 250 people were killed in just three months. The avalanches destroyed many villages and areas of forest. In recent years, early warning systems have been installed. An alarm is sent out if an avalanche is coming. This gives people some time to evacuate.

snowfall

heavy extra snow

sliding snow

90%
of people who die in avalanches caused the avalanche themselves.

Climate

The climate at high **altitudes** is different from the weather conditions in low areas. The higher the altitude, the colder and windier the weather.

Mountain peaks

The top part of most mountains sticks up high above the surrounding landscape. There is nothing of a similar height nearby to block strong winds or to trap warm air. This is why mountain peaks are extremely windy and cold. The light at high altitudes is also very intense, as the Sun's rays reflect off the snow.

Seasons

At the top of a mountain, the weather is cold all year round. The ice and snow at the peak may never melt. Lower down the mountain, there is more variety between the seasons. Winters are still cold, but there can be warm weather in the summer.

The snow at the peaks of the Himalayas never melts. Toward the base of the mountains, the climate is warmer and small plants can grow.

Shadows

Some parts of a mountain are always in shadow, as the high peak of the mountain blocks light from the Sun. This makes them much cooler than areas that receive sunlight. High mountain peaks can also create a rain shadow effect, as they block rain-carrying clouds.

The air cools near the mountains and clouds form.

Most of the rain from the clouds falls on the slope of the mountain that faces the sea.

When warm, moist air comes onto land from the ocean, it is carried inland by the wind toward mountains.

Less rain falls on the other side of the mountain. This area is in a rain shadow.

Oxygen

There is less oxygen in the air at high altitudes. Humans and animals need oxygen to survive. If there is less oxygen available, their bodies need to work harder than usual to keep healthy. This can make people feel ill and can even cause death (see page 24).

Death zone

Above 26,246 feet (8,000 m), there is not enough oxygen in the air for humans or most animals to survive. This area is known as the death zone. Cranes and whooper swans are among the few animal species that can survive in the death zone.

The summit of Mount Everest is in the death zone. Most people who climb to high altitudes on Everest breathe oxygen from tanks through masks.

Biomes

The landscape, climate, animals, and plants on a mountain change greatly depending on the altitude. There are many different **biomes** across mountainous areas.

Biome height

At the base of a mountain, there is often flat **grassland** or savanna. On the lower slopes, there are temperate forests made up of **deciduous** trees. Higher up, there is **taiga** forest with mainly **evergreen** trees. At around 9,842 feet (3,000 m) above sea level, the landscape changes to alpine **tundra**. The highest mountains have no plants at the top, just frozen ice and snow.

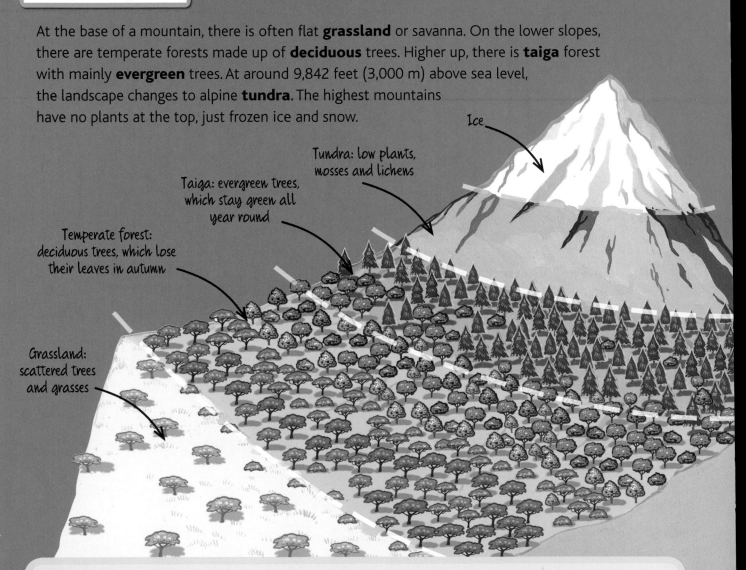

Ice

Tundra: low plants, mosses and lichens

Taiga: evergreen trees, which stay green all year round

Temperate forest: deciduous trees, which lose their leaves in autumn

Grassland: scattered trees and grasses

Treeline

The boundary between taiga forest and tundra is known as the **treeline**. This is the highest point at which trees can grow. Above this line, the temperatures are too low for trees to grow. Trees also can't get enough moisture from the soil, as any water is frozen into ice or snow.

Landscape

Near the base, mountains usually have gentle slopes covered with soil and plants. Higher up, there are more areas of jagged, exposed rock with some steep cliffs. It is much harder for animals and humans to climb over this rocky terrain. However, some mountain plant eaters, such as goats, are able to jump from rock to rock. They stay safe from predators by climbing steep slopes that other animals can't reach.

Animal and plant adaptations

Mountain animals have adapted to move around easily on the slopes. They need to be quick, with a good sense of balance. Plants have developed ways to protect themselves from the extreme conditions as well. Some grow hairs on their leaves to block intense sunlight. Many plants also grow low to the ground to avoid the strong winds.

The chamois has flexible hooves that help it scramble up rocky slopes.

The bristlecone pine grows incredibly slowly to conserve energy, as there are few nutrients in the rocky mountain soil.

The griffon vulture has good eyesight to spot dead animals lying on the mountainside, while it is soaring high above.

Extreme conditions

There are many dangers for humans on mountains. There is a risk of landslides and avalanches, or falling from a sheer drop. Extreme winds or freezing conditions can be life-threatening, too. However, these conditions can benefit mountain animals. It means that their habitats are mainly untouched by human activity such as hiking or hunting.

! Some insects manage to survive at great heights. There are bees and spiders that live above 18,044 feet (5,500 m) on Mount Everest. The spiders eat insects that have been carried up the mountainside by wind.

The Rocky Mountains

FACT FILE

LENGTH
3,000 miles (4,828 km)

HIGHEST POINT
**14,438 feet (4,401 m)
Mount Elbert**

COUNTRIES
Canada and the USA

The Rocky Mountains stretch inland along the west coast of North America. A wide range of animals and plants live in the biomes found at different altitudes.

Forests

The lower slopes of the Rocky Mountains are covered in temperate forests. Forests of pine and spruce trees, known as taiga or boreal, are found higher up. There is no clear division between temperate and taiga forests. They naturally blend together as the altitude increases.

Grassland

The bottom of valleys and slopes in the Rocky Mountains are covered in grassland. There are also large areas of grassland to the east of the Rocky Mountains, known as the Great Plains.

Twisted trees

Many of the trees at the very edge of the treeline in the Rocky Mountains grow in stunted, twisted shapes. This is because the very strong, icy winds kill higher branches. Lower branches are often sheltered by rock and snow. They grow in different directions to avoid the wind.

Twisted trees that grow high on mountains are also known as krummholz trees. Krummholz means bent wood in German.

Alpine tundra

Grasses and wildflowers grow in the alpine tundra above the treeline in the Rocky Mountains. In spring, the flowering plants bring color to the slopes. As the altitude increases, the number of plants decreases. The peaks of the Rocky Mountains are just exposed rock.

In this section of the Rocky Mountains in Utah, the layers of ice, tundra, and forest are clearly visible.

forest   ice   tundra

Predators

Large numbers of black bears live in remote forests across the Rocky Mountains. They mainly eat plants, but they will also hunt young deer and mountain goats. The gray wolf population is growing. Having a high number of gray wolves helps keep the forest biome in balance. The wolves' diet of elk and deer keeps the number of plant-eating animals from getting too high.

Sheep, deer, and elk

Elk and deer mainly live in the temperate forests and taiga, feeding on leaves and berries. Bighorn sheep (below) are surefooted enough to climb up to the alpine meadows. They graze on grass and live here in relative peace, away from forest predators.

Birds

ptarmigan

Birds of prey, such as owls and eagles, hunt in the forests and exposed rocky slopes of the Rocky Mountains. Above the tree line, ptarmigans feed on plants in the tundra. Ptarmigans grow white feathers in winter for camouflage against the snow.

! The Rocky Mountains are home to the bald eagle, the US national bird. In the past, the bald eagle population dropped dramatically due to hunting and deaths from pesticides. Recently, protection programs have helped the number of birds in the mountains to recover.

23

People and Mountains

At least 140 million people around the world have made their homes at or above 7,874 feet (2,400 m) above sea level. They have learned how to adapt to life on the inhospitable mountain slopes.

Villages

In some countries, conditions in mountain villages and towns can be tough. Unless it is grown in mountain valleys, food can be hard to come by. Supplies must be brought in. Villages often lack sewage systems and running water because it can be difficult to lay pipes through rock. Often there is no way to keep the water from freezing. If people suffer medical emergencies, they are far from doctors and hospitals.

La Paz in Bolivia is the highest capital city in the world. Some parts of the city are hard to access by car, so the city has installed a public cable car system.

Living at altitude

At high altitudes, the air has less oxygen and pressure. Less oxygen means your body has to work harder to breathe. People can feel dizzy, out of breath, tired, and get headaches. This is called **altitude sickness**. It is a problem for visitors to high altitudes. People who have lived at high altitude for many generations have adapted to life with much less oxygen. Scientists have observed that the bodies of these people are less affected by altitude sickness. Among other things, their lungs can breathe in and distribute more oxygen.

The highest permanent **settlement** in the world is La Rinconada in Peru, which sits at 16,732 feet (5,100 m) above sea level. Most of the town's 50,000 inhabitants were attracted to the town between 2001 and 2009 by jobs in the local gold mine.

Mountain activities

Many people travel to the mountains for holidays. Winter sports such as skiing and snowboarding attract many visitors to the slopes every year. All-year-round activities such as hiking and rock climbing are also popular.

Exploring mountains

In the 1800s, explorers from Europe and other other areas began trying to climb mountains around the world. The most difficult mountains to climb were the Himalayas and in particular, Mount Everest. Many famous climbers lost their lives trying to reach the summit of Everest. Finally, in 1953, New Zealander Sir Edmund Hillary and Nepalese Sherpa Tenzing Norgay made it to the top. There are still hundreds of mountains around the world where the summit has not been reached. They include the 24,835-foot (7,570-m) high Gangkhar Puensum in Bhutan.

Food

It is hard to grow food on steep mountain slopes. There is little flat land for farming, and the rocky soil isn't very **fertile**. Only certain crops, such as barley, quinoa, and potatoes, grow well in mountainous areas throughout the world.

! The boiling point of water gets lower as the altitude increases. This makes it harder to cook foods in water, as boiling water isn't as hot as it is at sea level!

Traveling up mountains

For some people, mountain climbing is a hobby, but for others, it's the only way for them to move around. It is hard to build roads and railways up mountain slopes, so people are forced to travel on foot. They use animals such as llamas, donkeys, or yaks to carry heavy loads.

Threats

High numbers of visitors threaten some fragile mountain regions. When people walk along and around mountain trails, they often drop litter, damage plants, and wear away rocks. This increases the risk of landslides. By making mountains into national parks, we can control the number of visitors and protect the habitat from future damage.

FOCUS ON The Himalayas

The Himalayan mountain range is home to some of the highest mountains in the world. Despite the high altitude, there are many small towns scattered across the Himalayas.

Lifestyle

Many people in the Himalayas work as farmers, raising livestock or growing crops. Many mountain villages and towns do not have running water, electricity, and sewage systems.

Tourism

There are advantages and disadvantages to tourism in the Himalayas. People can earn extra income by providing food and rooms for tourists. Some work as tour guides and others sell mountain crafts and souvenirs. However, large groups of tourists use more electricity and clean water, making life more difficult for local people who must conserve these resources.

Getting around

There are few roads high in the Himalayas. People have to carry food, medicine, and building supplies up the sides of the mountains. They use yaks to carry the heaviest objects and transport the rest on their backs. Some children have to walk and climb for many hours to get to school every day. A few children are sent to **boarding school** to avoid this problem.

FACT FILE

LENGTH
8,202 feet (2,500 km)

HIGHEST POINT
29,035 feet (8,850 m)
Mount Everest

COUNTRIES
Bhutan, India, Nepal, China, Pakistan, Afghanistan

Sherpas

People from the Sherpa ethnic group live in Nepal. They are expert mountaineers and are well known for their work as guides, assisting people who want to climb the Himalayas. The best-known Sherpa is Tenzing Norgay, who reached the top of Mount Everest in 1953, accompanied by Sir Edmund Hillary (see page 25).

These Sherpa men are carrying expedition supplies up to Everest Base Camp.

Mountain towns

Most people in the Himalayas live in small villages. However, there are also growing towns and cities. Some have been around for centuries, while others have grown larger because of tourism.

NAMCHE BAZAAR – 11,286 feet (3,440 m) *This village and trading hub is located in the Nepalese section of the Himalayas. It is a popular gathering point for climbers who are heading to the base camp on Mount Everest. They often stay for several days so that their bodies can adjust to the high altitude.*

LHASA – 11,975 FEET (3,650 m) *220,000 people live in the city of Lhasa in the Tibet Autonomous Region of China. It is one of the highest cities in the world and is filled with Buddhist temples and shrines, which attract many visitors. It is fairly easy to reach Lhasa, as it is connected to other settlements by roads, railways, and airlines.*

LEH – 11,482 FEET (3,500 m) *In the past, the town of Leh in India was an important trade center. It was in the middle of trading routes between the east and the west, so many traders passed through looking for food and shelter. The town is near the fertile Indus Valley. This makes it is easier for people to grow and buy a variety of foods.*

prayer flags

Religion

In the north of the Himalayas, most people are Buddhist. They build shrines and temples high in the mountains. Buddhists often hang colorful prayer flags high on mountain slopes, which they believe will bless the area. In the south, most people follow the Hindu religion.

Food and drink

Grains such as buckwheat, barley, and millet are some of the few foods that grow in the harsh climate of the Himalayas. These grains are ground into flour, which is used to make noodles and dumplings. People drink butter tea made with yak milk butter. This tea is high in calories, which people need to survive the cold weather.

butter tea

dumplings

Mountain Resources

Useful resources, such as rocks and trees, can be gathered from mountain slopes. People dig inside mountains to mine precious rocks and stones, which are sold at a high price.

Building materials

Mountain slopes are rocky. Rocks such as marble, limestone, and granite are used in construction. Large blocks of these rocks are cut away from the slopes in quarries. Later, they are cut into smaller pieces and used as flooring and wall coverings, and to make sculptures.

Mining

Some resources are found deep inside mountains. Miners dig down and use explosives in mines where copper, gold, and other metals are extracted. Mining can make mountains unstable, as the tunnels may not be able to support the weight of the rock above. This can result in the collapse of some areas of the mountain.

Large amounts of marble have been cut away from the slopes of these Italian mountains.

The Appalachian Mountains

The Appalachian Mountains are a mountain range in eastern North America. They are relatively low mountains that are rich in natural resources, such as coal and oil.

History

In the past, people mined coal underground in the Appalachian Mountains using pickaxes and explosives. This was dangerous, as it was hard to control the explosions. It took a large number of workers a long time to extract the coal.

Mountaintop removal

In the 1960s, people started using explosives to remove the tops of mountains. This left the coal inside the mountain exposed, so it could be easily cut away. The benefit of this was that fewer workers could extract more coal in safer conditions.

This photo shows the effects of mountaintop removal mining in the Appalachian Mountains.

FACT FILE

 LENGTH
1,988 miles (3,200 km)

 HIGHEST POINT
6,683 feet (2,037 m)
Mount Mitchell

 COUNTRIES
Canada, USA

Damage

Mountaintop removal mining has had a negative effect on the environment in the Appalachian Mountains. Many animals have lost their habitats when trees on the slopes were removed before the mountaintop removal mining. The trees were not replanted afterwards. Piles of rock from the mountaintops have been abandoned in nearby valleys. The mining has also affected the water supply in the area. Several rivers that began in the mountains have lost their **sources**. Dangerous chemicals and waste from the mines have poisoned the water and the land.

DANGER!

29

Glossary

altitude Height above sea level

altitude sickness Breathing problems and dizziness caused by not having enough oxygen due to high altitude

avalanche A large amount of snow, rock, and ice that falls down the side of a mountain

biomes Natural areas on Earth that have the same climate, landscape, plants, and animals

boarding school A school where students live and study

compression Pressing something into a smaller space

continental plate A large piece of Earth's crust that lies under a continent and along some coasts

convection current Movement caused by hot liquid rising and cool liquid falling

core The center of Earth

crust The outer layer of Earth

deciduous Describes trees that lose leaves in autumn and regrow leaves in spring

dense The molecules in a dense substance are closely compacted together

dormant Lying asleep, or inactive

erosion The process in which water and wind gradually wear away rock and soil

evergreen Describes trees that have leaves that stay green all year

extinct No longer active. Extinct volcanoes will not erupt again.

fertile Describes land where plants can grow well

glacier A large amount of ice that moves slowly

grassland A biome that is mainly covered in grass plants with few trees

landslide The movement of rocks and earth down a steep slope

lava Hot, melted rock outside a volcano

magma Hot, melted rock inside a volcano

mantle The layer of Earth underneath the crust

navigable Describes an area of water deep enough to sail a boat on

oceanic plate A large piece of Earth's crust that lies under the ocean

peak The top point of a mountain

plateau A large, flat, high area

plate boundary The place where two tectonic plates meet

sea level The height of the sea where it meets the land

settlement A place where humans have settled and live permanently, such as a town

source The place where a river starts

taiga A forest biome with mainly evergreen trees

tectonic plate A section of Earth's crust

treeline The maximum height where trees will grow on a mountain

tundra A cold biome with few plants that is covered by ice for most of the year

Test yourself!

1 How tall is Olympus Mons, the largest known mountain in our solar system?

2 What is the Earth's crust made from?

3 What is a dormant volcano?

4 Name two things that trigger avalanches.

5 Which biome is usually found above the taiga on mountainsides?

6 Who were the first people to reach the summit of Mount Everest?

7 Why is it hard to cook food at high altitudes?

8 Name two countries that the Himalayas pass through.

Check your answers on page 32.

Further reading

Mountains Around the World: The Himalayas
Molly Aloian (Crabtree, 2012)

Mountains Around the World: The Rockies
Molly Aloian (Crabtree, 2012)

Extreme Nature: Mountain Extremes
Gillian Richardson (Crabtree, 2009)

Websites

Read more about mountains at the following websites:

www.dkfindout.com/uk/earth/mountains/

www.ducksters.com/science/earth_science/mountain_geology.php

science.nationalgeographic.com/science/earth/surface-of-the-earth/mountains-article/

Index

Answers

1 15.5 miles (25 km)

2 Solid rock

3 A volcano that is unlikely to erupt again.

4 Some examples include earthquakes, heavy snowfall, and vibrations from human activity.

5 Tundra

6 Sir Edmund Hillary and Tenzing Norgay

7 Because the boiling point of water gets lower as the altitude increases, boiling water isn't as hot as it is at sea level.

8 Bhutan, India, Nepal, China, Pakistan, or Afghanistan